GROUNDCOVER
SERIES

To my wife Delyth and daughter Rebecca

Text research: David McDonald

Acknowledgements

I would like to thank staff at the following for their kind assistance
during the development of this book: West Dean Gardens,
Sackville College, Glyndebourne, Lewes Castle, The Royal Pavilion
(Brighton and Hove District Council), Brighton Pier and Fishbourne
Roman Palace.

I would also like to thank Malcolm Crampton
and Sarah Letts and all at Jarrold Publishing.

Geraint Tellem

Front cover picture: Brighton Pavilion
Back cover picture: Seven Sisters

Designed and produced by
Jarrold Publishing,
Whitefriars, Norwich NR3 1TR

All photographs © Geraint
Tellem and Jarrold Publishing

© Jarrold Publishing 2001

ISBN 0-7117-2019-3

Printed in Belgium.

1/01

PUBLISHER'S NOTE
Variant and archaic spellings have
been retained in quoted material,
while the modern spellings of
place-names have been used in
headings.
   The inclusion of a photograph
in this book does not necessarily
imply public access to the building
illustrated.

Brighton
and Sussex

GERAINT TELLEM

JARROLD
publishing

Arundel Cathedral

BRIGHTON
AND SUSSEX

GROUNDCOVER
SERIES

Sunset over Beachy Head

Contents

Map 10

Introduction 11

Brighton and Sussex 12

ACKNOWLEDGEMENTS 121

BIBLIOGRAPHY 122

INDEX 125

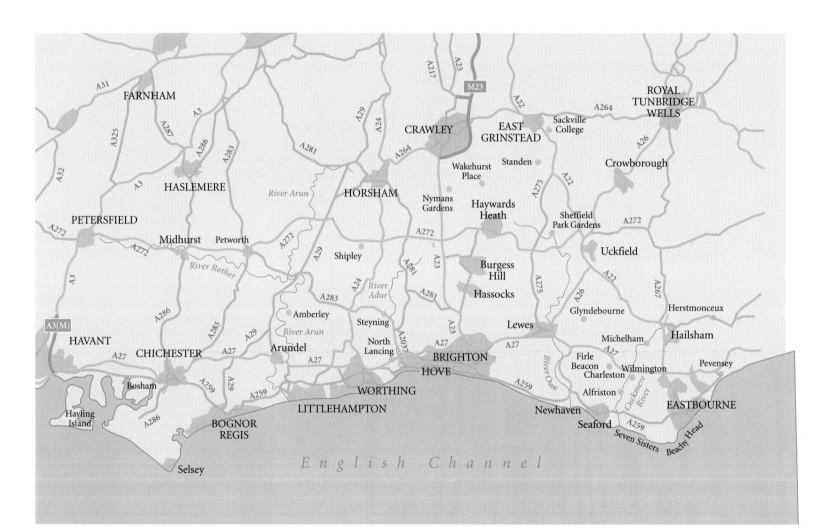

Introduction

Brighton typifies the traditional British seaside resort – the piers, the promenade, the funfairs and fishing-boats. Add to this the interesting shopping district of 'The Lanes', along with a lively and diverse cultural scene and this cosmopolitan town has something for everyone.

Brighton's popularity stretches back to the mid eighteenth century, when visitors flocked to the area to sample the purported health-enhancing properties of the sea, a practice championed by a local doctor. This time of change saw large-scale building development and produced terraces such as Regency Square, Adelaide Crescent and Kemp Town, and the Brunswick estate in neighbouring Hove. But the jewel in the crown is the unique Royal Pavilion, famous for its exotic Indian-style exterior and chinoiserie interior. This is a historic legacy of George IV, fondly known as 'Prinny', and the architecture dating from the period contributes to Brighton's unique character. With the arrival of the railway in 1841, tourism began in earnest and has flourished ever since.

Starting at the centre of Brighton, this book is a photographic tour that takes in the elements of this exuberant town before exploring the maritime county of Sussex.

The southern half of the county is dominated by the chalk escarpment of the South Downs, which sweeps to a dramatic conclusion at the cliffs of the Seven Sisters and Beachy Head. Further north, the Downs give way to the wooded landscape of the Weald, once the site of a thriving iron industry. The countryside is dotted with quintessentially English villages – thatched cottages and picturesque churches abound. Photographically one is spoilt for choice.

As well as spectacular scenery, Sussex boasts some of Britain's finest stately homes and gardens, notably Wakehurst Place, Nymans Gardens and Sheffield Park.

In the early part of the twentieth century many famous artists settled in the area, enticed by the peace and tranquillity. Charleston Farmhouse, near Firle, became a base for members of the Bloomsbury Group, while in 1902 author Rudyard Kipling made his home at Bateman's, where he completed much of his best work. Proximity to the continent has rendered Sussex vulnerable to invasion over the centuries, and the castles of Arundel, Pevensey and Lewes are testament to this turbulent past.

While working on this book I have found the many facets of Brighton and Sussex to be a constant inspiration. From the frolicsome atmosphere of Brighton Pier to the imposing grandeur of Beachy Head, this is a part of the British Isles I feel drawn to time and again.

Geraint Tellem

THE ROYAL PAVILION
BRIGHTON

We were quartered in the Pavilion, as the Regent's residence is called; it is decorated and furnished in the Chinese taste, and is illuminated by more than three thousand lamps of opalescent glass, which indeed give a really magnificent effect, but also produce an almost unbearable heat; the gallery is of quite unusual beauty . . .

ATTENDANT TO PRINCE LEOPOLD OF COBURG, ON THE OCCASION OF A ROYAL VISIT, 1816
Quoted in *Victoria History of the Counties of England: Sussex*, vol. 7
1973

THE ROYAL PAVILION
BRIGHTON

Pagodas salute us from
    London's high road,
For *à la Chinoise* is the taste
    à la mode.

POPULAR COUPLET PROVOKED BY THE
REBUILDING OF THE PAVILION IN 1817
Quoted in *Picturesque Sussex*
1910

THE ROYAL PAVILION
BRIGHTON

… the Royal Palace attracts
numbers who are puzzled to
know what to make of the
appearance of the building
which it is impossible for me,
or indeed any one else, to
describe.

MRS FITZHERBERT, 1819
Quoted in *Victoria History of the
Counties of England: Sussex*, vol. 7
1973

THE ROYAL PAVILION
BRIGHTON

To-day I have been going all over the Pavilion, which is really beautiful in its way. I did not think that the strange Chinese shapes and columns could have look'd so well. It is like Concetti in Poetry, in *outre* and false taste, but for the kind of thing as perfect as it can be, and the Prince says he had it so because at the time there was such a cry against the French things, etc., that he was afraid of his furniture being accus'd of Jacobinism.

LADY BESSBOROUGH, IN LETTER TO LORD GRANVILLE LEVESON GOWER, 1805
Quoted in CLIFFORD MUSGRAVE
Life in Brighton
1970

THE ROYAL PAVILION KITCHEN
BRIGHTON

That famous lady, Mrs Beeton, said the inhabitants of this county 'were noted for their savoury puddings.' There is a Sussex eel pudding, and almost anything can go into these puddings, rolled in a suet blanket and boiled in a cloth.

ESTHER MEYNELL
Quoted in *In Praise of Sussex*
1950

THE ROYAL PAVILION SOUTH GALLERY
BRIGHTON

Pugin relates an amusing incident which occurred while he was making sketches … He was engaged in one of the galleries of the Pavilion colouring a view. Deeply intent upon his drawing, he did not observe that someone had entered the apartment, but on looking round, to his surprise, saw the King, who was then advancing to the spot where he was sitting. Pugin had scarcely the time to rise when the King, passing by him and not perceiving a stool on which a colour-box was placed, accidentally overthrew it. The King stooped, instantly picked up the box, and gave it to Pugin with an expression of apology.

BENJAMIN FERREY
Recollections of A.N. Welby Pugin and his Father Augustus Pugin with Notices of their Works
1861

GEORGE IV STATUE
BRIGHTON

It is the fashion to run down George IV, but what myriads of Londoners ought to thank him for inventing Brighton!

WILLIAM MAKEPEACE THACKERAY
From 'The Four Georges'
lectures 1855–7

THE ROYAL PAVILION
BRIGHTON

It was in the year 1824, while Nash was engaged in building the Pavilion at Brighton, that he received the King's command to prepare a work illustrating that extraordinary Hindu structure. Mr Nash naturally requested Pugin to take sketches, make the drawing, and superintend the engraving …

BENJAMIN FERREY
Recollections of A.N. Welby Pugin
and his Father Augustus Pugin
with Notices of their Works
1861

BRIGHTON PIER AND **BEACH**

Watch the pebbles on the beach; the foam runs up and wets them, almost before it can slip back the sunshine has dried them again, so they are alternately wetted and dried. Bitter sea and glowing light, bright clear air, dry as dry – that describes the place.

RICHARD JEFFRIES
Quoted in *In Praise of Sussex*
1950

BRIGHTON PIER AND WEST PIER

The West Pier was opened in October 1866, having taken three years to build at a cost of £30,000. The structure was designed by the engineer Eusebius Birch, who also built the Aquarium some years later … The West Pier was always celebrated for its sideshows, which included in June 1890 a display of performing fleas.

CLIFFORD MUSGRAVE
Life in Brighton
1970

BRIGHTON PIER

… The Palace Pier has set the standard of gaiety and elegance for piers … all over the world.

CLIFFORD MUSGRAVE
Life in Brighton
1970

Brighton Pier was formally known as Palace Pier.

THE LANES
BRIGHTON

In its Victorian heyday
Brighton had over 470 pubs
and beer shops that catered
for summer visitors. The
town was alive with the
bustle of minstrel shows,
conjurors, performing
monkeys and canaries, and
string bands, with street
vendors selling cakes, ginger
beer and brandy balls adding
to the colourful scene.

BRIGHTON

Brighthelstone was
    confess'd by all
T'bound with females
    fair,
But more so since
    fam'd Russell has
Preferred the waters
    there.

WILLIAM KEMPE
Quoted in CLIFFORD
MUSGRAVE
Life in Brighton
1970

ROYAL CRESCENT
BRIGHTON

This group of houses was the first ever planned in Brighton as a single architectural composition, and was an audacious conception for its time, as well as being today one of the most attractive features of the sea-front, the houses having charming classical doorways, ironwork balconies and bonnet-like balconies, and being faced with the black, iridescent, glazed 'mathematical' tiles that create such delightful effects in the changing lights of the sky.

CLIFFORD MUSGRAVE
Life in Brighton
1970

ST PETER'S CHURCH
BRIGHTON

The new parish church of St Peter at Brighton, built . . . in the time of George IV, from 1824 to 1828, was not only one of the very first manifestations of the new movement of religious fervour in this country, and one of the very first early nineteenth-century churches to be built in Gothic style, but also one of the most beautiful. Charles Barry [the architect] used Gothic with the serenity and purity of the classical spirit in which he had been trained, and his tower of St Peter's, built of dazzling white Portland stone, soars out of the valley of the Steine at the junction of the London and the Lewes roads, offering its beauty to the visitor from either direction . . .

CLIFFORD MUSGRAVE
Life in Brighton
1970

STREET LAMPS
BRIGHTON

The Pavilion grounds were the first part of town to be lit with the new illuminant [gas], . . . By no means all the inhabitants were in the favour of the new illuminant, which was regarded by some as dangerous and unhealthy. However, on a vote being taken at a public meeting held in May 1818, 400 persons were found to be in favour and only 150 against.

CLIFFORD MUSGRAVE
Life in Brighton
1970

THE LANES
BRIGHTON

When the town was rebuilt after the burning by the French, the new houses were in many places re-erected on the site of the old, and it is indeed possible that some of the ancient flint and pebble walls of buildings in the Lanes, in parts of great thickness . . . may date back to medieval times, but most of the houses date from the eighteenth and early nineteenth centuries.

CLIFFORD MUSGRAVE
Life in Brighton
1970

METROPOLE HILTON
BRIGHTON

The Metropole Hilton was designed by Alfred Waterhouse, the architect who also designed the old Hove Town Hall and the Natural History Museum in London. This elegant Victorian hotel sits in a prime position on the seafront of the town, within walking distance of Brighton's famous 'Lanes', shopping centre, theatre and restaurants.

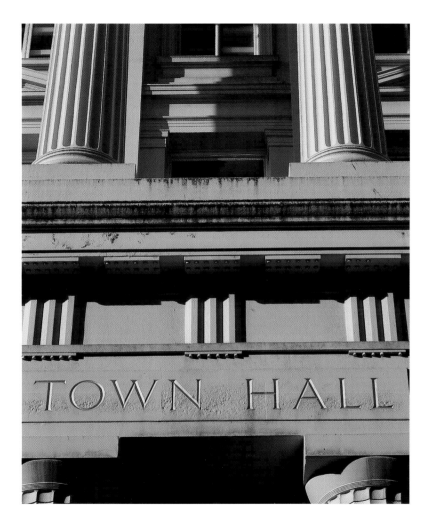

TOWN HALL
BRIGHTON

[In 1773, by Act of Parliament] Control of paving, lighting, and cleaning the streets, of the market and fairs and of weights and measures, and powers to build groins and a town hall were given to the [new Town] commissioners, who were empowered to levy 6*d*. a chauldron on all coal brought into the town by sea . . . The new hall in Market Street was built by the commissioners in 1830 at a cost of £60,000, largely at the instance of Thomas Read Kemp.

Victoria History of the Counties of England: Sussex, vol. 7
1973

BRIGHTON

Brighton became considerably
more prosperous in the 1750s
when Dr Richard Russell,
a physician from Lewes,
established sea-bathing and
medicinal spring cures, ensuring
the town's popularity as a spa
resort.

CHICHESTER
TERRACE
KEMP TOWN

A visit to Brighton comprised
every possibility of earthly
happiness.

Jane Austen
Pride and Prejudice
1813

THE CRICKETERS
BRIGHTON

A famous local cricketer called Jutten acquired
the inn in 1790 and altered its name from the
'Laste and Fishcart'. It was then close to the old
fishmarket, a laste being a measure of fish.
The house, first known as an inn in 1547, is
in appearance at least Dickensian, three storeys
tall, with bow-shaped fronts and curved
windows … The early Victorian interior is
pleasing and warm and comfortable and, as
befits the new name of the inn (dating merely
from 1779), the bar pictures have a cricketing
flavour among the brasses.

RODNEY L. WALKERLEY
Sussex Pubs
1966

GRAND HOTEL
BRIGHTON

The Grand Hotel was built in the Italianate
style between 1862 and 1864. The scale of
the building and the opulence of its exotic
interiors, inspired by oriental design and
art, ensured that it lived up to its name.

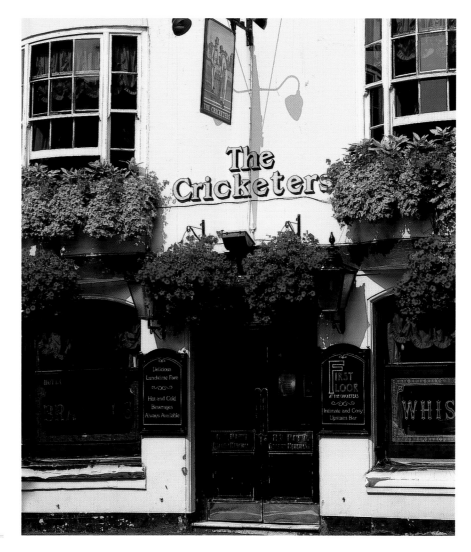

BATH ARMS, THE LANES
BRIGHTON

Brighton is a beautiful town on the coast, quite new and much frequented by fashionable society for the sake of sea-bathing.

ATTENDANT TO PRINCE LEOPOLD OF COBURG, ON THE OCCASION OF A ROYAL VISIT, 1816 Quoted in *Victoria History of the Counties of England: Sussex*, vol. 7 1973

HISTORY OF BATH ARMS

The Bath Arms is the oldest licensed premises actually in the original lanes, established around 1864 having previously been two cottages - one a fruit shop and the other owned by John Burridge, a hat and cap maker.

Before the present day array of shops and restaurants arrived, the lanes were a warren of fishing cottages, merchants and small tradesmen. At this time the pub was known as The True Briton Eating and Beer House, changing to The Bath Arms in 1868.

Deep in the cellar is a bricked up old tunnel which connects with a maze of underground passages under the lanes.

Now restored to its former glory the Bath Arms offers visitors a taste of true British heritage and hospitality in congenial surroundings at the heart of the historical lanes.

T&J BERNARD

THE LANES
BRIGHTON

The area of the Old Town famous as The Lanes was at the centre of Brighton in medieval times. The narrow, twisting passages and alleys were called 'twittens'. The Market Inn was formally a hotel called The Golden Fleece.

THE LANES
BRIGHTON

One of the best physicians
our city has ever known, is
kind, cheerful, merry
Doctor Brighton! Hail, thou
purveyor of shrimps, and
honest prescriber of South
down mutton!

WILLIAM MAKEPEACE THACKERAY
From 'The Four Georges' lectures
1855–7

BRIGHTON MARINA

The marina at Black
Rock was opened to the
public in July 1978 and
is the largest marina in
Europe. Its 127 acres
(51 ha) accommodate
some 1,500 boat
moorings and a small
fishing fleet, as well as
a multiplex cinema
and a pub.

BRUNSWICK SQUARE
HOVE

The ground to the west of the town, where Brunswick Square and its twin terraces now stand, [used to be] devoted to the growing of flax for the making of linen thread and cloth. No one living in Brighton early in the eighteenth century could have dreamed that in no more than a hundred years the sea-front of the town would present one of the most magnificent façades in Europe, consisting of a panorama nearly three miles long of stately white stucco or iridescent black tiles; pediments and porticoes, columns and pilasters.

CLIFFORD MUSGRAVE
Life in Brighton
1970

BRUNSWICK SQUARE
HOVE

The estate of Brunswick Town, which incorporated Brunswick Square and Brunswick Terrace, was inspired by the development of Kemp Town. Building began in 1824, and in 1830 a board of commissioners was appointed to regulate the estate's housing, church and closed market.

BRUNSWICK TERRACE
HOVE

One of the chief delights of Brighton and Hove, its 'West End', is the magnificent seaboard prospect of open Regency terraces and squares ...

RONALD F. JESSUP
Sussex
1949

ADELAIDE CRESCENT
HOVE

Building of Adelaide Crescent began in 1830 with the construction of ten houses. However, 50 years elapsed before more houses were added and the difference in style between the older and newer buildings can be clearly seen.

NEWTIMBER HILL
SOUTH DOWNS

Broad and bare to the skies
The great Down-country lies,
Green in the glance of the sun,
Fresh with the clean salt air;
Screaming the gulls rise from
    the fresh turned mould,
Where the round bosom of
    the wind-swept wold
Slopes to the valley fair.

ROSAMUND MARRIOTT WATSON
Quoted in *In Praise of Sussex*
1950

POYNINGS

The old name for this parish was Punnins, and the modern spelling is still pronounced Punnings. It is a beautiful spot, possessing a long record in history. The church was founded by one of the De Ponynges, who dying in 1369, had added to his will: 'I demise to him who may be my heir, a ruby ring, which is *the charter of my heritage of Poynings*, together with the helmet and armour which my father demised to me.'

CLARE JERROLD
Picturesque Sussex
1910

POYNINGS

The exceptionally fine and cruciform church (Holy Trinity) was built under the terms of the will of Michael, third Lord Poynings, who died in 1368, and has been very little altered since. For its date and compared with the nearby contemporary churches of Etchingham and Alfriston, it has singularly few traces of the lingering Dec. style. These are in fact confined to the font and the central tower.

RONALD F. JESSUP
Sussex
1949

DEVIL'S DYKE

Why the 'Devil's Dyke'? Legend says the Devil
intended to dig a dyke across the valley to let in
the sea to flood the people and churches of the
Weald; but an old woman lit her lamp at night,
and the Devil, believing it was dawn, stopped
digging and fled – thus the area was saved.

CECILE WOODFORD
Portrait of Sussex
1984

LANCING COLLEGE CHAPEL

Lancing is popularly said to take its name from
Wlencing, second son of the Saxon invader Aella.
. . . Lancing College on the hill-slope to the north,
is one of a famous group of Church of England
public schools founded by the late Canon
N. Woodward in 1848. [Its] noble chapel …
a very beautiful building, quite dominates
its surroundings

RONALD F. JESSUP
Sussex
1949

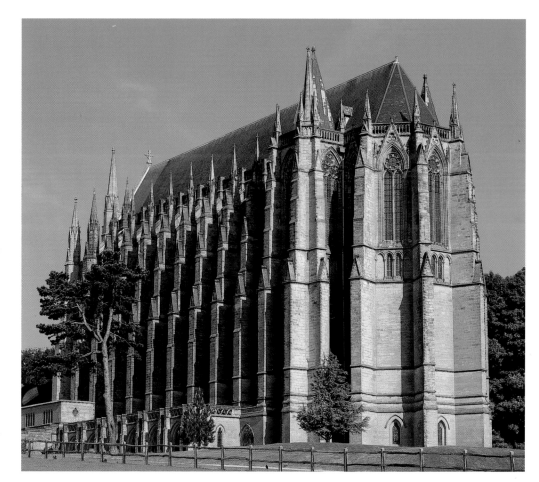

ST NICHOLAS' CHURCH
BRAMBER

Built partly as a chapel to the castle and given to the abbey of St Florent at Saumur *c.* 1075. The building must date from the very first few years after the Conquest or rather, what is left of it; for it shared both the general decline of the town and the particular depredation of the C17. It was used as a gun emplacement for attacking the castle in 1642.

IAN NAIRN AND NIKOLAUS PEVSNER
Sussex
1965

BRAMBER CASTLE

The mound looks as though it might be a gargantuan motte, like Ongar or Thetford, but is in fact natural. On top of it [is] a smaller motte (pre-Conquest) and then a huge fragment of a tower-keep which served also as a gatehouse.

IAN NAIRN AND NIKOLAUS PEVSNER
Sussex
1965

STEYNING

These 'Wealden' houses represent perhaps the finest expression of medieval house design… most appear to have been built by the rising class of yeoman farmers and by successful traders and craftsmen … Over the county as a whole many have been recognised in recent years concealed behind later façades or additions, or uncovered during actual demolition of what had been assumed to be a quite different type of building.

J.R. ARMSTRONG
A History of Sussex
1995

ARUNDEL CASTLE

… How that chap Riggs was banging the car up this hill – the deuce of a hill, too, past chalk-pits and gravel pits, and grassy down and dipping spurs of covert, past the lodge of a park, into a great beech-wood. Very pretty – very still – no life but trees, spreading trees, very cool, very green! Past a monstrous great church thing, now, and a lot of high walls and towers – Arundel Castle.

JOHN GALSWORTHY
Swan Song
1928

ARUNDEL CASTLE

Since William rose and
    Harold fell
There have been Earls
    of Arundel,
And Earls old Arundel
    shall have
While rivers flow and
    forests wave.

Old rhyme quoted in CLARE JERROLD
Picturesque Sussex
1910

ARUNDEL CASTLE

If ever a foreigner asks me to
show him something which
is typically English, I shall
run him down to Arundel
and walk him through
the park.

H.V. MORTON
I Saw Two Englands
1943

ARUNDEL CATHEDRAL

The Catholic church was built by the 15th Duke of Arundel and was completed in 1872. In 1965 it was rededicated to become the Cathedral Church of Our Lady and St Philip Howard. St Philip was the 13th Earl of Arundel who converted to the Catholic faith following the execution of the Jesuit martyr Edmund Campion. In 1585 Philip was imprisoned for his faith in the Tower of London and died there ten years later. He was canonised in 1970 and his remains are enshrined in the cathedral.

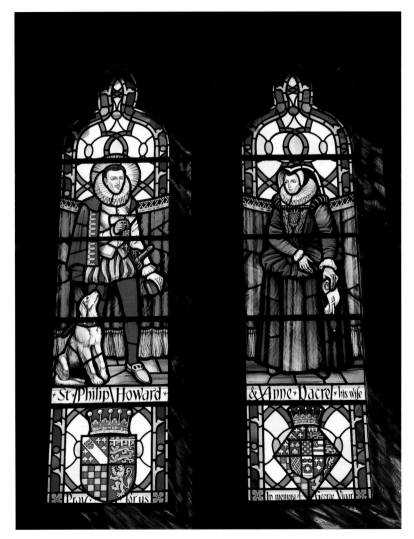

BOGNOR REGIS

The history of Bognor practically begins with Sir Richard Hotham, a London hatter who had made a fortune in trade. Attracted by the climate and the benefit which he had received from sea-bathing, he bought a farmhouse and enlarged it, as 'Bognor Lodge', in 1797 and started to convert the district into a watering place.

Victoria History of the Counties of England: Sussex, vol. 4
1973

BOGNOR REGIS
DOME

The Dome House, which still stands, Sir Richard [Hotham] built … in 1799 in the hope of attracting King George III to stay there. The king did not come, but in 1808 his granddaughter the young Princess Charlotte came there and remained for two years …

Victoria History of the Counties of England: Sussex, vol. 4
1973

SELSEY

King Ethelwalch of the
South Saxons, gave to the
most reverend Prelate
Wilfred, land of eighty-
seven families to maintain
his company who were in
banishment, which place is
called Selsey, that is, the
island of the seals . . .

THE VENERABLE BEDE
Quoted in J.R. ARMSTRONG
A History of Sussex
1995

SELSEY

It is believed that the name
Selsey is a derivation of
'Seal Island'. The peninsula
was an island until the end
of the nineteenth century
when construction of the
causeway began. In more
recent times Selsey
experienced a tornado on
7 January 1988 which was
reported worldwide.

CHICHESTER CATHEDRAL

If Chichester steeple fall
In England there's no king at all.

ANCIENT LOCAL PROVERB
Quoted in CLARE JERROLD
Picturesque Sussex
1950

CHICHESTER CATHEDRAL

The fair little cathedral city of one
of the fairest counties in England
. . . the cathedral at the heart of it
set in its ring of trees, its long
white lines and its silver roof, its
noble towers and its dainty spire,
all mingling in this lovely scene.

ARTHUR MEE
Quoted in *In Praise of Sussex*
1910

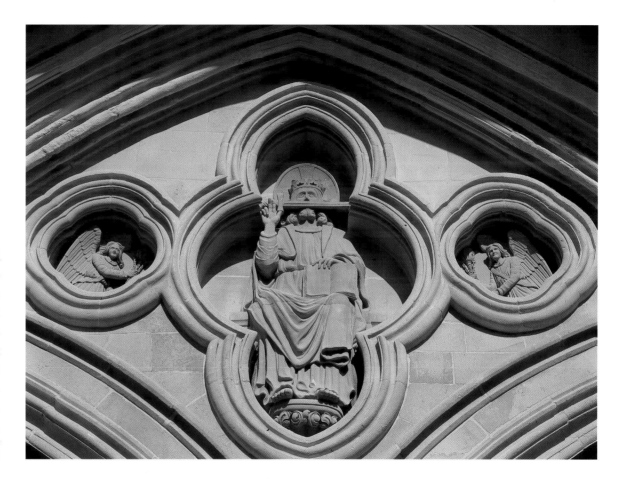

MARKET CROSS
CHICHESTER

Chichester's elaborate
market-cross, fifty feet high,
and adorned with arches,
flying buttresses and
bannerets, was built about
1500 by Bishop Storey, that
the poor might trade there
without paying dues. It
was much defaced by
Parliamentarians, and
now, by some irony of
circumstance, the one niche
filled contains a bust of
Charles I.

CLARE JERROLD
Picturesque Sussex
1910

CHICHESTER

Chichester is the
administrative centre of
West Sussex and has been
prominent since the Romans
established the market town
of *Noviomagus*. Remains of
Roman occupation can be
seen at nearby Fishbourne
Roman Palace. Today,
Chichester remains a
prosperous and thriving
town that boasts some
fine Georgian architecture
and beautiful merchants'
houses.

CHICHESTER CATHEDRAL

The bell tower at Chichester Cathedral was built around 1400 to house the great bells from the central tower. Although other cathedrals had detached towers, only Chichester can boast an original that has survived from the medieval period.

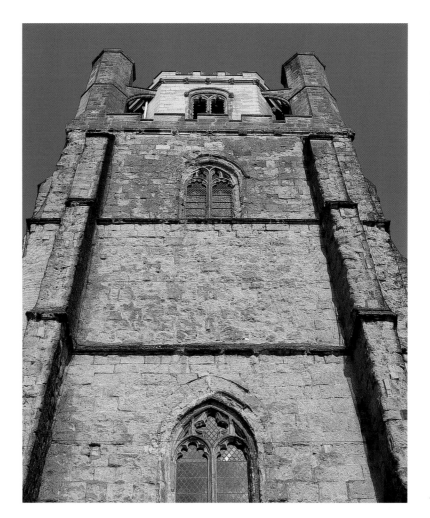

ROMAN PALACE
FISHBOURNE

Fishbourne Roman Palace was discovered in 1960 when workmen laying a waterpipe uncovered a mosaic; excavation of the site has revealed one of the most significant Roman buildings in Britain. It is believed that the palace was built around AD 70 with the exquisite mosaics added at various stages over the next two centuries. The original building would have been very grand indeed.

BOSHAM

About three miles to the west of
Chichester, on an inlet of the sea
known as Chichester Harbour,
lies the little town of Bosham . . .
It is now a fishing village,
beautiful and glittering when the
sea flows around it at high tide . . .

CLARE JERROLD
Picturesque Sussex
1910

BOSHAM

From its church marauding Danes
once stole the tenor bell, and put out to
sea; but the bell refusing to remain
with them, sank through the ship into a
deep hole in the harbour, and is said
that even now, when the other bells
ring, this one can be heard chiming in
from the depth of the sea.

CLARE JERROLD
Picturesque Sussex
1910

WEST DEAN GARDENS

The splendid park contains in a natural chalk bowl a fine arboretum which is open to the public on certain days during the rhododendron season each spring.

RONALD F. JESSUP
Sussex
1949

FITTLEWORTH

Fittleworth to the east, beloved of artists, who have lavishly decorated the walls of the inn, is in the midst of tempting woods, and was built many years ago, so that its houses seem one with the landscape, giving no shock of incongruity to the beholder.

CLARE JERROLD
Picturesque Sussex
1910

AMBERLEY

Amberley is one of the loveliest and friendliest of Sussex villages. It lies on the slightly rising ground at the foot of the Downs on the left bank of the Arun, from which it is separated by a wide marsh known as Amberley Wild Brooks.

RONALD F. JESSUP
Sussex
1949

HALNAKER MILL

Halnaker Mill is one of Sussex's most distinctive and best-loved landmarks. Standing majestically on top of the downs it is visible for miles around and is often used for navigation at sea; during the Second World War it was a military observation tower. The mill was built in 1740 and was completely restored during the 1950s.

STOPHAM BRIDGE

An idyllic spot, with what is easily the best of the medieval bridges in Sussex. Rebuilt in stone in 1423. The raised centre arch dates from 1822, the others are original – six low, obtusely pointed arches with blunt cutwaters between. The rhythm of arch and cutwater, and of the overall line of the bridge, from bank to bank, could hardly be improved upon.

Ian Nairn and Nikolaus Pevsner
Sussex
1965

NYMANS GARDENS

Of copses still with dreams,
Of pinewoods stark, red-
    stemmed, and tall,
Of purple wastes of ling,
Lanes that the sunlight
    only sees
In a dapple of shifting
    tapestries,
Haunted lakes where the
    moor-hens call,
And hills where the mad
    larks sing.

A.F. BELL
Quoted in *In Praise of Sussex*
1950

NYMANS GARDENS

Nymans Gardens was
created by four generations
of the Messel family into a
30-acre (12-ha) space that
includes collections of rare
plants, trees and shrubs.
The sculpted feel of the
garden juxtaposes with the
190 acres (77 ha) of wood-
land and wild garden.

WAKEHURST PLACE

The seat of the Wakehurst and Culpeper families was Wakehurst Place built by Sir E. Culpeper in 1590, and although it has been altered considerably it is regarded as the best example in Sussex of a late Elizabethan house.

RONALD F. JESSUP
Sussex
1949

The house replaced an earlier mansion on the Wakehurst estate.

WAKEHURST PLACE

The Culpeper family first became associated with the Wakehurst estate and its family in 1454 when two Culpepers married the last remaining Wakehursts. Nicholas Culpeper, the famous physician and herbalist, was a member of another branch of the Culpeper family.

WAKEHURST PLACE

To lie on a warm bed of South Down
thyme is to understand how the
ultimate compliment paid by the
Greeks to an author was that his
verses smelt of thyme.

MARCUS WOODWARD
Quoted in *In Praise of Sussex*
1950

The gardens at Wakehurst are leased
to the Royal Botanic Gardens at Kew
by the National Trust. The rich
collection is comprised of exotic
trees, plants and shrubs from
around the world. Flora from
Tasmania, south-east Asia, Australia
and the Himalayas contrast with the
formal ornamental style of this
English garden.

SACKVILLE COLLEGE

… to bestow on the building thereof the sum of one thousand pounds or such a sum as shall be necessary, and to endow the same with a rent-charge of £330 a year out of my lands, etc.; towards the relief of one-and-thirty unmarried persons, 21 men and 10 women there to live, to pray, serve, honour and praise Almighty God.

ROBERT SACKVILLE,
2ND EARL OF DORSET,
WHO DESIGNED SACKVILLE
COLLEGE IN 1609 TO PROVIDE
A COLLEGE OR HOSPITAL

SACKVILLE COLLEGE

The principal purpose of Sackville College has not changed since its foundation by Robert Sackville. However, the beautiful Jacobean building is open to the public during the summer months.

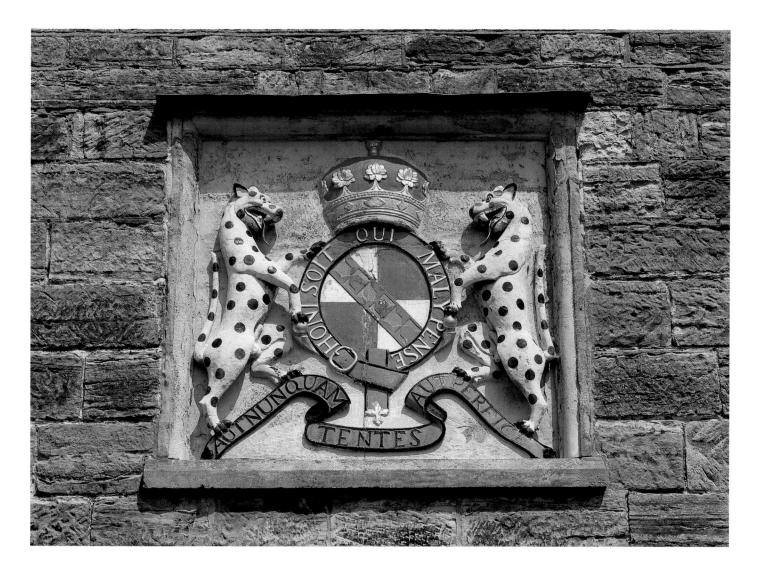

SACKVILLE COLLEGE

A previous warden at Sackville was the Reverend John Mason Neale, the composer of 'Good King Wenceslas' and other well-known hymns.

STANDEN HOUSE

Built at the end of the nineteenth century, Standen House is a treasure house of carpets, wallpapers and fabrics in the distinctive Arts and Crafts style. The house was designed around existing buildings by Philip Webb. His meticulous attention to detail coupled with his flair and imagination have culminated in a uniquely charming testament to the skill of traditional craftsmanship.

SHEFFIELD PARK

I worked for Lord Sheffield at Sheffield Park an' it was a very big estate. There was fourteen groundsmen, twelve kitchen-garden staff and twenty farmhands. We had six gamekeepers an' a boy as well as the head-keeper… When I was learnin' I used t' go out with the head-keeper, Pritchard, ferretin'. We'd leave about nine in the mornin' with about a hundred nets an' we always reckoned to have about a hundred rabbits before dinner at one.

Quoted in B. COPPER
Across Sussex with Belloc
1995

BATEMAN'S
NEAR BURWASH

The dwelling … is solidly constructed of blue-grey stones overgrown with creepers and roses … Around is a delightful garden, and near by a quaint oast house, formerly used for brewing but now converted into a cottage for the accommodation of guests.

ERNEST H. RANN
The Homeland of English Authors
1927

Bateman's was the home of the writer Rudyard Kipling from 1902 until his death in 1936. The property is now owned by the National Trust.

HASTINGS

The tradition is that the old town of Hastings is swallowed up by the sea. That which standeth now is couched between a high cliff to seaward and as high a hill landward . . . the haven, such as it is being fed but with a poor, small rill is at the south end of the town . . .

WILLIAM CAMDEN
Quoted in J.R. ARMSTRONG
A History of Sussex
1995

PEVENSEY CASTLE

[Pevensey Castle] is one of the best preserved of the Sussex ruins, though in the sixteenth century an order was issued that it should either be re-edified or utterly razed! In 1650 the materials were sold for £40, the purchaser, however, mercifully leaving them standing . . . Pevensey fell before the terrible siege of Ella the Saxon, who in taking it 'slew all that dwelt therein, nor was there one Briton left'. It has since been four times besieged, by Earl Godwin, by Rufus, by de Montfort, and by the adherents of Richard II.

CLARE JERROLD
Picturesque Sussex
1910

HERSTMONCEUX CASTLE

Herstmonceux is a splendid sight. The house is large, the moat wide, and the brick colour is a wonderful soft red in the lush surrounding green.

IAN NAIRN AND NIKOLAUS PEVSNER
Sussex
1965

HERSTMONCEUX CASTLE

The castle of Herstmonceux was built by Sir Roger de Fienes … between 1440 and 1447 … one motive was certainly defence against a French landing on the flat Pevensey levels which the castle commands … it was inspired by continental models – in this case the use of brick was copied from the Flanders region. Herstmonceux was in fact the first building of any size to be built of this material in England since Roman times. Flemish brickmakers and bricklayers had to be brought over to supervise the work.

J. R. ARMSTRONG
A History of Sussex
1995

BODIAM CASTLE

Bodiam Castle, on the Rother, though little more than a shell, stands proudly in the midst of its lily-covered moat, its ten towers, round and square, being about seventy feet in height. Inside are to be found the remains of the hall. Chapel, and kitchen, the latter with two fireplaces and oven of tiles. It was built on the site of a weaker building by Sir Edward Dalyngruge, a warrior of Poitiers.

CLARE JERROLD
Picturesque Sussex
1910

MICHELHAM PRIORY

Michelham Priory [in Upper Dicker, is] a stone-built house incorporating remains of a priory of Augustinian canons founded in 1229 by Gilbert de Aquila of Pevensey. It is pleasantly placed on the edge of a common and a most delightful part of the River Cuckmere . . .

CECILE WOODFORD
Portrait of Sussex
1984

THE LONG MAN OF WILMINGTON

The Great White Man of Wilmington must surely be one of the best-known images in Europe. Cut in the face of the Downs … he is 240 feet in length with a staff in each hand, and outlined in white bricks on the green turf of Windover Hill, rising 600 feet above sea level … The Long Man's origin still remains a mystery . . . Perhaps the Saxon's made him – or he may have been there 1,000 years earlier. Others believe him to be the work of the Wilmington monks. Perhaps the mystery of its origin is best preserved …

CECILE WOODFORD
Portrait of Sussex
1984

BEACHY HEAD

With giant-port high
   towering o'er the
   main,
Beachy, thy cliffs in
   massy grandeur rise
Like some cleft castle,
   which with calm
   disdain
Still braves the outrage of
   inclement skies ...

THOMAS PARK
Quoted in *In Praise of Sussex*
1950

BEACHY HEAD

Eastbourne's glory is
Beachy Head, the last of
the Downs, which stop
dead at the town and
never reappear in
Sussex again.
(The name Beachy
has nothing to do
with the beach: it is
derived probably
from the Norman's
description – 'beau
chef'.) About Beachy
Head one has the South
Downs in perfection:
the best turf,
the best prospect,
the best loneliness,
and the best air.

E.V. LUCAS
Highways and Byways in Sussex
1950

SEVEN SISTERS

I well remember one particular downland day – a summer's day which unfolded just as any other on those faraway childhood holidays. Out of the dusk a lark sprang up, soaring above the darkness, singing incessantly. From the fields of the little farmstead where we were staying near West Dean towards the famous Seven Sisters cliffs the white light of dawn splashed along the ridge of cliffs.

CECILE WOODFORD
Portrait of Sussex
1984

CUCKMERE HAVEN

None of the Sussex rivers in this day have a wild and torrential character – they crawl gently along through peaceful stretches of meadowland, past willows and rushes and cows pasturing on their banks . . . Anyone looking down from High-and-Over on the wide valley of the Cuckmere can hardly believe that valley was carved through the chalk barriers by that gentle thread of river.

ESTHER MEYNELL Quoted in *In Praise of Sussex* 1950

ALFRISTON

Like a few other Sussex pubs …
the Star Inn at Alfriston might
be taken for a stage set for a
medieval drama … The upper
storey is faced in plaster with
upright timbering, pierced by
three oriel lead-lighted windows
that jut out above your head, and
the village cratfsman of many
centuries ago has left his wood
carvings with heraldic arms,
snakes, a robed bishop, a reveller
with bottle and flask, St Michael
in combat with a dragon (the
dragons lurked in Sussex forests
long before the Romans came)
and kindred pleasantries.

RODNEY L. WALKERLEY
Sussex Pubs
1966

CHARLESTON FARMHOUSE

Charleston was once the home of the artists Duncan Grant, Clive Bell and Vanessa Bell. The farmhouse was frequented by members of the Bloomsbury Group, including Vanessa Bell's sister, Virginia Woolf, the artist Dora Carrington and T.S. Eliot. Over a period of 60 years, Grant and the Bells hand-decorated the interior of this building.

FIRLE BEACON

Though I have now travelled the Sussex Downs upwards of thirty years, yet I still investigate that chain of majestic mountains with fresh admiration year by year; and I think I see new beauties every time I traverse it. The range, which runs from Chichester eastward as far as East-Bourn, is about sixty miles in length, and is called the South Downs, properly speaking, only round Lewes. As you pass along, you command a noble view of the wild, or weald, on the one hand, and the broad downs and the sea on the other.

GILBERT WHITE
Natural History and Antiquities of Selborne
1789

GLYNDEBOURNE

The old part is pre-Tudor and still
contains a little contemporary panelling.
The Opera House, added in 1934, seats
600 people and has a stage of continental
size and equipment. Its noted annual pre-
war Mozart Festival is expected to
develop considerably in the future.

RONALD F. JESSUP
Sussex
1949

The original Opera House closed in
1992 and in 1994 a magnificent
new building was opened.

GLYNDEBOURNE

Glyndebourne was founded by
John Christie, a science teacher and
opera-lover who was married to an
opera-singer. He inherited the
Tudor mansion at Glyndebourne
and built the world-famous opera
house to indulge his enthusiasm.

JILL WINDMILL

A very well-known pair [of windmills] on the brow of the Downs about 5 miles north of Brighton at Clayton are … preserved as landmarks. The post mill is 'Jill' and is, in fact, equipped with all its machinery, and after years of being idle is now being restored. 'Jack', the Tower Mill has recently had sweeps added by a film company …

CECILE WOODFORD
Portrait of Sussex
1984

LEWES CASTLE

Of all the towns in Sussex, perhaps there is not one which history has made so romantic as its capital, Lewes … It is built in terraces upon a steep hill, which is crowned by the ruined castle …

CLARE JERROLD
Picturesque Sussex
1910

LEWES

Lewes Castle, now approached by a turning called Castle Gate in High Street, was peculiar in having had two keeps – one called Brack – built upon artificial mounds, at a distance of 800 feet from each other. The gate-house is early Edwardian, but the original Norman archway still remains within. A great wall enclosed the two mounds, upon one of which only the foundations of the ancient tower are left.

CLARE JERROLD
Picturesque Sussex
1910

LEWES

It is very beautiful when you get on to the brow of the hill above Falmer: a long way off to the right you can see Lewes lying like a box of toys under a great amphitheatre of chalk hills: the whole ride is very pleasant: Lewes, when you get there, lies on a ridge in its valley, the street winding down to the river [Ouse] which runs into the sea at Newhaven: on the whole it is set better than any town I have seen in England.

WILLIAM MORRIS
Quoted in CLARE JERROLD
Picturesque Sussex
1910

DITCHLING

Here the Romans made a camp and dug a road deep enough to send an army unperceived into the low land of the Weald. Partly by this old way we may descend into Ditchling, which in spite of its antiquity, or perhaps because of it, is still a small village. On its common rises a chalybeate spring, once much patronised for rheumatism, but now ignored.

CLARE JERROLD
Picturesque Sussex
1910

NEWTIMBER HILL

O bold majestic downs,
    smooth, fair and lonely;
O still solitude, only
    matched in the skies;
Perilous in steep places,
Soft in level races,
Where sweeping in
    phantom silence the
    cloud-land flies;
With lovely undulation of
    fall and rise;
Entrenched with thickets
    and thorned,
By delicate miniature dainty
    flower adorned!

ROBERT BRIDGES
Shorter Poems
1913

Herstmonceux Castle

Acknowledgements

Every effort has been made to secure permissions from copyright owners to use the extracts of text featured in this book.

Any subsequent correspondence should be sent to Jarrold Publishing at the following address: Jarrold Publishing, Whitefriars, Norwich NR3 1TR.

page

13   Reproduced from the *Victoria County History, Sussex, Volume 7*, by permission of the General Editor.

14   (left) *Picturesque Sussex* by Clare Jerrold. 'The Shire Series', S. Combridge, 1910.

14   (right) as page 13.

17   *Life in Brighton* by Clifford Musgrave. Faber & Faber Ltd, 1970. Reproduced by kind permission of the publisher.

18   *In Praise of Sussex*, compiled by Neville Hilditch. Frederick Muller Ltd, 1950. Reproduced by kind permission of the publisher.

22   As page 18.

25   As page 17.

26   As page 17.

29   As page 17.

30   As page 17.

33   As page 13.

37   *Sussex Pubs* by Rodney L. Walkerley. B.T. Batsford Ltd, 1966. Reproduced by kind permission of the publisher.

38   As page 13.

43   (left) As page 17.

44   *Sussex* by Ronald F. Jessup. Methuen Publishing Ltd, 1949. Reproduced by kind permission of the publisher.

47   (right) As page 18.

48   (left) As page 14.

48   (right) As page 44.

51   (top) *Portrait of Sussex* by Cecile Woodford. Robert Hale, 1984. Reproduced by kind permission of the publisher.

51   (bottom) As page 44.

53   *Sussex* by Ian Nairn and Nikolaus Pevsner. Penguin, 1965. Reproduced by kind permission of Penguin Ltd.

54   *A History of Sussex* (3rd edition) by J.R. Armstrong. Edited by Richard Pailthorpe and Diana Zeuner. Phillimore & Co. Ltd, 1995. Reproduced by kind permission of the publisher.

57   *Swan Song* by John Galsworthy. Heinemann, 1928. Reproduced by kind permission of the publisher.

58   (left) As page 14.

58   (right) *I Saw Two Englands* by H.V. Morton. Methuen Publishing Ltd, 1943. Reproduced by kind permission of the publisher.

63   Reproduced from the *Victoria County History, Sussex, Volume 4*, by permission of the General Editor.

64   As page 54.

67   (top) As page 14.

67   (bottom) *The King's England – Sussex* by Arthur Mee. Reproduced by kind permission of the King's England Press Ltd.

68   (left) As page 14.

73   As page 14.

74   As page 44.

77   (left) As page 14.

77   (right) As page 44.

78   (right) As page 53.

81   (left) As page 18.

83   (left) As page 44.

85   As page 18.

91   *Across Sussex with Belloc* by B. Copper. Sutton Publishing Ltd, 1995. Reproduced by kind permission of the publisher.

92   *The Homeland of English Authors* by Ernest H. Rann. Methuen Publishing Ltd, 1927. Reproduced by kind permission of the publisher.

94   (left) As page 54.

94   (right) As page 14.

97   (top) As page 53.

97   (bottom) As page 54.

99   (top) As page 14.

99   (bottom) As page 51 (top).

101   As page 51 (top).

102   (left) As page 18.

102   (right) *Highways and Byways in Sussex* by E.V. Lucas. Macmillan, 1950. Reproduced by kind permission of the publisher.

104   (left) As page 18.

104   (right) As page 51 (top).

106   As page 37.

112   (top) As page 44.

115   (left) As page 51 (top).

115   (right) As page 14.

116   As page 14.

118   (left) As page 14.

Bibliography

Ainsworth, Harrison: *Ovingdean Grange: A Tale of the South Downs.* Herbert Jenkins, 1928.

Armstrong, J.R.: *A History of Sussex* (3rd edition). Edited by Richard Pailthorpe and Diana Zuener. Phillimore & Co. Ltd, 1995.

Austen, Jane: *Pride and Prejudice.*

South Gallery, Royal Pavilion

Penguin, 1994.

Bridges, Robert: *Shorter Poems.* George Bell & Sons, 1913.

Cobbett, William: *Rural Rides.* Penguin, 1967.

Copper, B.: *Across Sussex with Belloc.* Alan Sutton, 1995.

Ferrey, Benjamin: *Recollections of A.N. Welby Pugin and his Father Augustus Pugin with Notices of their Works.* Edward Stanford, 1861.

Galsworthy, John: *Swan Song.* Heineman, 1928.

Hudson, W.H.: *Nature in Downland.* Longmans, Green & Co., 1906.

In Praise of Sussex, ed. Neville Hilditch. Frederick Muller Ltd, 1950.

Jerrold, Clare: *Picturesque Sussex, 'The Shire Series'.* S. Combridge, 1910.

Jessup, Ronald F.: *Sussex.* Methuen Publishing Ltd, 1949.

Lucas, E.V.: *Highways and Byways in Sussex* (revised edition). Macmillan, 1950.

Mee, Arthur: *The King's England – Sussex.* Hodder & Stoughton, 1943.

Meynell, Esther: *Sussex.* Robert Hale, 1949.

Morton, H.V.: *I Saw Two Englands.* Methuen Publishing Ltd, 1943.

Musgrave, Clifford: *Life in Brighton.* Faber & Faber Ltd, 1970.

Nairn, Ian and Pevsner, Nikolaus: *Sussex.* Penguin, 1965.

Rann, Ernest H.: *The Homeland of English Authors.* Methuen Publishing Ltd, 1927.

Swinburne, Algernon: *Collected Poetical Works.* Heineman, 1927

Thackeray, William Makepeace: *The Four Georges: Sketches of Morals, Manners, Court and Town Life.* Smith, Elder & Co., 1866.

Victoria History of the Counties of England: Sussex, vol. 4, 1973.

Victoria History of the Counties of England: Sussex, vol. 7, 1973.

Walkerley, Rodney L.: *Sussex Pubs.* B.T. Batsford Ltd, 1966.

White, Gilbert: *Natural History and Antiquities of Selborne.* Appleton, 1898.

Wilkinson, Walter: *A Sussex Peep Show.* Geoffrey Bles, 1933.

Woodford, Cecile: *Portrait of Sussex.* Robert Hale Ltd, 1984.

Above: The Rotunda, Petworth House
Opposite: West Pier, Brighton

Index

Alfriston 106
Amberley 77
Armstrong, J.R. 54, 64, 94, 97
Arun, River 77
Arundel 56–61
    Castle 11, 56–8
    Cathedral 6, 61
Austen, Jane 34

Barry, Charles 29
Bateman's 11, 92
Beachy Head 8, 11, 102
Bede, The Venerable 64
Beeton, Mrs 18
Bell, A.F. 81
Bell, Clive 108
Bell, Vanessa 108
Bessborough, Lady 17
Birch, Eusebius 24
Bloomsbury Group 11, 108
Bodiam Castle 99
Bognor Regis 63
    Dome House 63
Bosham 73
Bramber 52–3
    Castle 53
    St Nicholas' Church 53
Bridges, Robert 118
Brighton 11–41
    Bath Arms 38
    Black Rock 41
    Brighton Marina 41

Brighton Pier 11, 22, 24, 25
Brighton Beach 22
Cricketers, The 37
Grand Hotel 37
Kemp Town 11, 34, 43
Lanes, The 11, 26, 30, 33, 38, 40
Market Inn 38
Market Street 33
Metropole Hilton 33
Regency Square 11
Royal Crescent 29
Royal Pavilion 11, 13–19, 21, 30
St Peter's Church 29
Town Hall 33
West Pier 24

Camden, William 94
Campion, Edmund 61
Carrington, Dora 108
Charles I, King 68
Charleston Farmhouse 11, 108
Charlotte, Princess 63
Chichester 66–70
    Cathedral 67, 70
    Harbour 73
    Market Cross 68
Christie, John 112
Clayton 115
Cuckmere
    Haven 104
    River 99
Culpeper family 83

Dalyngruge, Sir Edward 99
de Aquila, Gilbert 99
de Fiennes, Sir Roger 97
de Montfort, Simon 94
Devil's Dyke 51
Ditchling 118

Eastbourne 102, 111
Eliot, T.S. 108
Ella the Saxon 94
Ethelwalch, King 64

Ferrey, Benjamin 19, 21
Firle 11
    Beacon 111
Fishbourne Roman Palace 70
Fittleworth 77
Fitzherbert, Mrs Maria 14

Galsworthy, John 57
George III, King 63
George IV, King 11, 19, 21, 29
Glyndebourne 112
Godwin, Earl 94
Grant, Duncan 108

Halnaker Mill 78
Hastings 94
Herstmonceux Castle 97
High-and-Over 104
Hotham, Sir Richard 63
Hove 11, 42–7
    Adelaide Crescent 11, 47
    Brunswick Square 43
    Brunswick Terrace 44
    Brunswick Town 11, 43
    Old Town Hall 33

Jeffries, Richard 22
Jerrold, Clare 48, 68, 73, 77, 99, 115, 116, 118
Jessup, Ronald F. 44, 48, 51, 74, 77, 83, 112
Jill Windmill 115

Kemp, Thomas Read 33

Kempe, William 26
Kipling, Rudyard 11, 92

Lancing College Chapel 51
Leopold, Prince of Coburg 13, 38
Leveson Gower, Lord Granville 17
Lewes 115–17
    Castle 11, 115, 116
Lucas, E.V. 102

Mee, Arthur 67
Messel family 81
Meynell, Esther 18, 104
Michelham Priory 99
Morris, William 116
Morton, H.V. 58
Musgrave, Clifford 24, 25, 29, 30, 43

Nairn, Ian 53, 78, 97
Nash, John 21
National Trust 85, 92
Neale, Revd John Mason 88
Newtimber Hill 47, 118
Nymans Gardens 11, 81

Ouse, River 116

Park, Thomas 102
Pevensey 99
    Castle 11, 94
Pevsner, Nikolaus 53, 78, 97
Poynings 48
Pugin, A.N.W. 19, 21

Rann, Ernest H. 92
Richard II, King 94
Rother, River 99
Royal Botanical Gardens Kew 85
Russell, Dr Richard 26, 34

Sackville, Robert 86
Sackville College 86, 88
St Philip Howard 61
Selsey 64
Seven Sisters 11, 104
Sheffield Park 11, 91
South Downs 11, 47, 111
Standen House 88
Steine valley 29
Steyning 54, 55
Stopham Bridge 78
Storey, Bishop 68
Sussex Weald 11, 118

Thackeray, William Makepeace 21, 41

Upper Dicker 99

Wakehurst family 83
Wakehurst Place 11, 83, 85
Walkerley, Rodney L. 37, 106
Waterhouse, Alfred 33
Watson, Rosamund Mariott 47
Webb, Philip 88
West Dean 104
    Gardens 74
White, Gilbert 111
Wilfred, Prelate 64
William II, Rufus, King 94
Wilmington, Long Man of 101
Woodford, Cecile 51, 99, 101, 104, 115
Woodward, Marcus 85
Woodward, Canon N. 51
Woolf, Virginia 108

Opposite: Bosham

GROUNDCOVER
SERIES